THE WHITE SOX

A Pictorial History

THE WHITE SOX

A Pictorial History

Richard Whittingham

Contemporary Books, Inc.
Chicago

Library of Congress Cataloging in Publication Data

Whittingham, Richard, 1939–
    The White Sox: a pictorial history

    1. Chicago White Sox (Baseball team)   I. Title.
GV875.C58P34   1980   796.357'64'0977311   81-69624
ISBN 0-8092-5769-6   AACR2

Acknowledgments

The author and publisher would especially like to thank the following organizations for their help and cooperation in putting this book together: the Chicago White Sox, especially Chuck Shriver and Ken Valdiserri of the public relations department and owners Ed Einhorn and Jerry Reinsdorf; the National Baseball Hall of Fame in Cooperstown, New York; and the Chicago Historical Society.

All photos are reproduced through the courtesy of the Chicago White Sox unless otherwise specified.

Published by Contemporary Books, Inc.
180 North Michigan Avenue, Chicago, Illinois 60601
Manufactured in the United States of America
Library of Congress Catalog Card Number: 81-69624
International Standard Book Number: 0-8092-5769-6

Published simultaneously in Canada by
Beaverbooks, Ltd.
150 Lesmill Road
Don Mills, Ontario M3B 2T5
Canada

Contents

Prologue

Comiskey Park was primed and polished for the return of major league baseball on August 21, 1981. For two long summer months it had been a relic, standing gaunt and empty like the Coliseum in Rome. But the players' strike was over and in the late afternoon there were stirrings inside the huge stadium. Ushers milled about the grandstands waiting for the gates to open, vendors and concessionaires were busy with the preliminary logistics of their trade, and the groundskeepers were putting the last touches on the infield. Finally the White Sox players ambled out onto the field for batting practice and the traditional rites of loosening up. It was humid and overcast, and the threat of rain was very real, but two hours before game time the parking lots that surrounded the ballpark were filling and the fans were already queued up outside or at McCuddy's bar across 35th Street.

This particular night was important because it was the first White Sox home game in the second half of the 1981 baseball season. The Yankees, always a draw, were in town. Their roster was gilded with million-dollar names like Reggie Jackson, Dave Winfield, Graig Nettles, and Ron Guidry as well as a bevy of stars who once wore Sox uniforms—Bucky Dent, Eric Soderholm, Jim Spencer, Oscar Gamble, Tommy John, and Rich "Goose" Gossage. Besides that, the White Sox were soaring. They were returning from a road trip with a record of 9–6 and an undisputed grip on first place in the American League East.

Up in the press box, Harry Caray, Jimmy Piersall, and Lou Brock were telling the Chicago radio audience how good it felt to be back. Former Yankee great, Phil Rizzuto was in the next booth briefing New York radio listeners about what was to transpire in Comiskey Park that night. Minnie Minoso moved among the beat reporters and sports columnists, the compleat ambassador of goodwill for the Sox.

The gates opened at 5:45 and immediately fans were pushing through the turnstiles. Within minutes the quiet echoes of the near-empty stadium were washed away in a flood of noise. Those creating the cacophony were the real fans; at the park early to watch batting practice, to shout encouragement and shriek dissatisfactions, and to talk with one another about the nuances of the game and the particularities of the White Sox of 1981. It was a scene that has been played and replayed in the same ballpark for more than 70 years. Those making the noise and voicing their opinions in 1981 were little different than the fans who came out to watch the game when Fords were Model T's and the president was Woodrow Wilson. They were just as ardent as the fans who cheered the picture-perfect hitting of Shoeless Joe Jackson and Eddie Collins,

1

the masterful pitching of Ed Walsh and Red Faber, and watched with respect as Ray Schalk calmed the nerves of countless pitchers. The devotion was the same for the team owned by Eddie Einhorn and Jerry Reinsdorf as it had been for the one run by the Old Roman himself, Charles A. Comiskey.

Looking down at the playing field within the walls of the house Comiskey built, any nostalgia buff could easily conjure visions of Ted Lyons working his wizardry from the mound, or Luke Appling fouling off pitch after pitch until he drew the walk he wanted, or Nellie Fox with that enormous chaw of tobacco in his mouth, or Luis Aparicio—under the thunderous chant of "Go-Go-Go"— stealing second base, or Bill Veeck—wooden leg and all—masquerading as a returning hero of the Revolutionary War, or home runs sailing into the stands from the bats of sluggers like Pat Seerey, Gus Zernial, Eddie Robinson, Bill Melton, Richie Allen, and Richie Zisk.

The stadium is different now from what it was in earlier days. There is a scoreboard that occasionally erupts with earshattering explosions and sends fiery pyrotechnic displays into Chicago's southside sky. The grass has gone from natural to artificial turf and back again. And the ballplayers who run on it collect considerably more dollars for their efforts. There may be designated hitters and intra-league playoffs today, but the game itself has changed little in the more than 100 years that it has been played professionally in America.

And that's what the fans are there for this steamy August night—more than 30,000 of them. They are not at Comiskey Park simply to watch the hype that is part of the hometown launch of Part 2 of the 1981 season. They pay little attention to the models in newly designed team uniforms parading around the stadium. They smile benignly at the introduction of the team's two new mascots, take-offs of the famous San Diego chicken man. A pre-game burst from the scoreboard which sounds a little like the siege of Bastonne does not interrupt conversations or cause anyone to spill his beer. What brings them to their feet and animation to their vocal chords is the game itself. And even the rain delays that will come this sultry night do not dim the enthusiasm.

The White Sox take the field, the names on Tony LaRussa's roster have not been forgotten during the strike's hiatus, they're all there—Lemon, LeFlore, Almon, Squires, Fisk, Luzinski, Nordhagen, Lamar Johnson. Britt Burns is on the mound and he sets the mighty Yankees down one after the other. In the sixth inning he has a no-hitter going until Dave Winfield spoils it with a clean single to left. The superstitious crowd, having refrained from jinxing him by talking about a possible no-hitter, gives Burns a standing ovation for his performance preceding that hit. The Yankees take a 1–0 lead. But in the eighth inning the White Sox come back. There are runners on first and second when slugger Carlton Fisk comes to bat. But, fine hitter that he is, there will be no heroics for him that night. He gets the sign to bunt and dumps a perfect roller down the third base line and the runners move easily to second and third. As Fisk trots back to the dugout after his sacrifice, the fans are on their feet cheering as if he had just sent a game winning shot over the left field fence. Greg Luzinski comes to the plate next. Massive, powerful, he is a Chicago boy who has finally come home to play. And this night, this at bat, he finds his pitch. The report of bat meeting ball reverberates across the field. The ball screams out to left, a line drive pulling sharply toward the foul line marker. But it stays fair and crashes into the stands like a bazooka shell. The Sox take a 3–1 lead. Again, the fans roar their approval.

And then the rains come. The players and umpires trot off the field, the tarpaulin is rolled out over the infield, the fans in the lower seats move quickly to the ramps under the stadium, the dedicated stay and gaze out at the teeming rain that dances in the glare of the stadium lights. Up in the press box the media members and other hangers-on break up into conversational groups. Down on the deserted field the rain forms a pattern of ponds on the plastic tarp and shows no sign of letting up.

Finally the game is called. The White Sox get the win, and they remain in first place. Those who have stayed now head for the dry comfort of their cars or the buses and els. It is nearly midnight when the players shower and the Sox front office personnel start laying the plans for the game the following night. It will be a mere 20 hours until the same pageant will take place to the same chorus of cheers and groans . . . as it has so many times on summer days and summer nights for the White Sox since they were born more than 80 years ago.

1—
The Early Years

The White Sox came to Chicago with the turn of the century. In 1900, William McKinley was president of the United States and Carry Nation was storming saloons with her hatchet in hand. It was the year of only the second modern Olympic Games and a mere 10 years since Dr. James Naismith had invented the game of basketball. There was no NFL, NBA, NCAA, or NHL. James J. Jeffries was the heavyweight champion of the world. Red Grange, Bobby Jones, and Jesse Owens hadn't even been born and Jack Dempsey, Bill Tilden, and Paavo Nurmi were just little boys who had yet to start to school.

In the first month of the 20th century, Charles A. Comiskey, owner and manager of a minor league franchise in St. Paul, brought his club from Minnesota to the city of Chicago to join the newly formed American League. The idea for the new baseball league was the brainchild of Ban Johnson, the president of the minors' Western League. He wanted to launch another major league, one to compete on the same ground as the well-established National League.

In 1900, however, his league was still minor. But it was well organized. Besides Chicago, AL teams had homes in Milwaukee, Indianapolis, Detroit, Kansas City, Cleveland, Buffalo, and Minneapolis. And the owners of all of them had their collective eye on playing *major* league baseball very soon.

The White Sox were known as the "White Stockings" back then and their ballpark was on the old Chicago Cricket Club grounds at 39th and Wentworth. Their debut at that park was April 21, 1900, and 5,200 fans came out to watch them. They lost 5–4 in 10 innings to a Milwaukee team managed by Connie Mack. But they went on to win 82 games that inaugural year against 53 losses (.607), enough to earn the first American League Championship. (They ended up four games ahead of the second-place Milwaukee club.) The most remarkable performance of the year was the four straight shutouts by White Stocking pitcher Jack Katoll, all identical 3–0 wins.

The American became a major league the following year and from that moment on, Chicago was home to two big league franchises. There were eight teams in each major league in 1901, and although the AL was an accepted reality there would be no World Series until 1903.

Many of the stars of the NL defected to the fledgling AL that first year. Chicago enticed 31-year-old Clark Griffith to take the mound for them and to manage the team. Other greats who abandoned the Nationals included Cy Young, Nap Lajoie, John McGraw, and Iron Man Joe McGinnity. Still the National League kept such name players as Christy Mathewson, Rube Waddell,

Kid Nichols, Wild Bill Donovan, Wee Willie Keeler, Ed Delahanty, Frank Chance, Jesse Burkett, and Sam Crawford.

The White Stockings gained the distinction of having played the first game in American League history, an honor they would have been forced to share had the games scheduled for Baltimore, Detroit, and Philadelphia not been rained out that day. In Chicago, however, the sun shined on April 24th and the American League was launched before 14,000 fans out on Chicago's South Side. There was music from the Rough Riders Band, the ceremony of throwing out the first ball, and the announcement that the team's name was being abbreviated to "White Sox."

The White Sox won the pennant that maiden year of the American League. Clark Griffith posted 24 victories for them and lost only seven games. Roy Patterson was another 20-game winner. Fielder Jones, who played right field, led the team with a .311 batting average and third baseman Fred Hartman was only two percentage points behind him. First baseman Frank Isbell stole 52 bases, the most in either league that year, and the team itself—perhaps the original "Go-Go Sox"—led the majors with a total of 280 base thefts. When the season ended, the White Sox had a record of 83–53 (.610), this time four games in front of the runners-up from Boston.

Cy Young won 33 games for Boston in the AL that year, the most in either league. And Nap Lajoie of Philadelphia was the first AL triple crown winner—batting .422, hitting 14 homers, and driving in 125 runs. After it was over, there was little doubt that the American League would be able to live comfortably and profitably with the older National League, who as a result of the trespass of the AL had rather joylessly celebrated its 25th anniversary.

Life at the top was short for the Sox, however. They dropped to fourth place in 1902 and plummeted to seventh the following year. Clark Griffith departed the team just before the 1903 season to go to New York and manage a new franchise that was to become known as the Yankees. Although they were declining, the Sox were still exciting to watch: A base-stealing team with one of the finest fielding units in the league. They just couldn't hit very well. Fielder Jones and Danny Green were the only consistent hitters, near or above .300. As for slugging in those early years, the most the team as a whole could produce in one season was 14 home runs.

Doc White became a member of the Sox pitching staff in 1902, Nick Altrock and Frank Owen joined him in 1903, and Big Ed Walsh arrived in 1904. All would engrave their names on early White Sox pitching records. Another hurler, Patsy Donovan, would earn the ignoble distinction in 1903 of being the first Sox pitcher to lose more than 20 games in a season (his record, 11–25).

The White Sox and the Cubs played their first interleague series in 1903, a 14-game affair held after the regular season. Chicago baseball fans of either persuasion equally shared the joys and woes of it as the Sox and Cubs won seven games each. It would become an autumn tradition that would not come to an end until the war years of the 1940s.

By 1904, the Sox were on their way back up—to third place anyway—on the arms of 21-game winners Nick Altrock and Frank Owen, and 16-game winners Frank Smith and Doc White, as well as some very fleet feet on the basepaths (the team's 216 thefts were the league high and no less than 10 players stole 11 bases or more). Fielder Jones had taken over the managerial tasks midway through the season, although he still held court in center field as well. Ed Walsh in his rookie season was relatively unimpressive, with a 5–5 record, but Old Roman Comiskey said he had "great faith in that young man's potential."

It would not be until 1906, however, before the Sox would return to the top. The year before, they made a strong bid for the pennant, narrowly losing out in the closing days of the season to a Philadelphia team whose fortunes had been guided by two devastating pitchers, Rube Waddell and Eddie Plank. The next year, however, it would be a story with a happier ending for Sox fans.

They were called the "Hitless Wonders," those White Sox of 1906, but they managed to win the American League pennant with a record of 93–58 (.616) despite a team batting average of .230 and slugging average of .286, both being the lowest in the league. The Sox only hit six home runs the entire year, and Fielder Jones was the premier slugger with two roundtrippers.

Still they were there, the AL representative in baseball's third World Series. It would come to be called the "Trolley Series" because it was played in one city and fans could commute back and forth between the Cubs west side park and the Sox field on the South Side via Chicago's venerable trolley cars. It also would come to stand as Chicago's only intra-city World Series.

The Cubs were a heavy favorite. They had won a grand total of 116 games in 1906 and lost only 36 (.763). Both records—most wins and highest win percentage in a season—still stand today. They had the famous infield combination of Joe Tinker, Johnny Evers, and Frank Chance. They boasted a pitching staff which included Mordecai "Three Finger" Brown, Ed Reulbach, and Jack Pfiester, who won 65 games among them. The Cubs team batting average of .262 was 32 percentage points higher than that of the Sox.

But baseball is unpredictable and the 1906 Series certainly was a cogent example of that. Everything was unexplainably juxtaposed, suddenly there was a Cub team that could not hit and a Sox team that could. It took six games for the White Sox to win it, and in the last two the once weak Sox offense scored eight runs in each game and knocked out a total of 26 hits in the two slug-fests. Big Ed Walsh won two games (one a shutout), and Nick Altrock and Doc White got wins in the other two. There was another factor as well: The managerial acumen of Fielder Jones who, as one writer of the day put it, "made all the right decisions and none of the wrong ones."

When it was over, there was little question that Ed Walsh had emerged as the team's premier pitcher. A big man, especially in those days (6'1", 220 pounds), he would reinforce his pitching reputation the following year with 24 wins and a league-leading ERA of 1.60. To say Walsh was an iron man on the mound is an understatement. He pitched and won both games of a doubleheader in 1908, and in 1907 and 1908 he pitched in 56 and 66 games, often with no more than two days rest. In 1908, he won 40 games, by far the most in White Sox history.

The Sox, however, were not as lustrous as Walsh in the years that followed their World Series victory. They dropped to third place in 1907 and 1908, then to fourth, and finally sixth, as the Detroit Tigers behind the hitting of Ty Cobb and Sam Crawford, and the pitching of Wild Bill Donovan and George Mullen came to dominate the American League in the second half of the century's first decade.

Pitching and fielding were not Sox problems in those years. In fact in those categories the team often led the league. Hitting was the real void. In 1908, the team hit only *three* home runs all season, a major league low which never has and surely never will be removed from the record books. In 1909, they hit four and the following year zoomed to seven. The team batting average was as low as .211 (1910) and at best was only .237 (1907). Fans remained loyal, however, and in 1907 alone the Sox led both leagues in home attendance (666,307).

At the end of the decade, the Sox got a new home. The stadium was built on the corner of 35th and Shields. For $100,000, Old Roman Comiskey had bought a 600×600-foot lot there from the estate of Chicago's first mayor, John Wentworth. Formal groundbreaking was held in the middle of February 1909 and the first game was played on July 1, 1910. The architect was Zachary Taylor Davis, who would later design Wrigley Field as well, and his plans called for a seating capacity of 35,000—6,400 box seats, 12,600 grandstand seats, and wooden-bench bleachers to accommodate 16,000. The original dimensions were 362 feet along each foul line and a long 420 feet to dead center field. The cost of construction was somewhere in the vicinity of $500,000. It was formally called White Sox Park; Comiskey's name would not be inscribed on it until later in the decade.

New stadium or not, the Sox remained a mediocre ball club for the next six years. It would not be until 1916 before there would be anything that could be described as pennant fever on Chicago's south side. Since Fielder Jones had retired from managing the Sox in 1908, the club had gone through three managers—Billy Sullivan, Hugh Duffy, and Nixey Callahan—but the team still went steadily down during those years (1909–1914). Clarence "Pants" Rowland took over in 1915 and the tide was jarringly reversed. He managed to take a sixth-place team with a won-lost percentage of .455, which had ended up 30 games out at the end of the season, and turned it into a third-place team with a .604 percentage of wins, which trailed the league-leading Boston Red Sox by only 9½ games.

Before Pants Rowland arrived, however, the Sox made some of the most propitious acquisitions in the team's history. First, they purchased the services of pitcher Eddie Cicotte from the Red Sox. Then came catcher Ray "Cracker" Schalk from the Milwaukee minor league club. In 1913, Urban "Red" Faber was brought up from Des Moines. And the infield jewel, Ed "Cocky" Collins, destined to be one of the game's greatest stars, signed on after the 1914 season.

By 1915, the White Sox actually could boast of a team hitting threat. Eddie Collins batted .332 that year, second only in the AL to Ty Cobb's .369. In addition, Sox first baseman Jack Fournier hit .322, third best in the AL, and his slugging average of .491 was highest in the league. The Sox team total of 25 home runs was second best.

The following year the White Sox stayed in the thick of the pennant race all the way to the wire, only to lose out in the final days to the Boston Red Sox. (The pennant winners of 1916 were spurred by a pitcher named Babe Ruth who won 23 games for them and led the league with an ERA of 1.75.) For the White Sox, three batters hit above .300. Shoeless Joe Jackson, who had been acquired from Cleveland the season before, led the team with .341, trailing only Tris Speaker (.386) and Ty Cobb (.371) in the AL. Eddie Collins hit .308 and Oscar "Happy" Felsch came in at a respectable .300 in his sophomore year in the major leagues. Shoeless Joe also led the majors in triples with 21, a White Sox team record which still stands today.

But it was 1917 that was destined to be the year of the White Sox. Babe Ruth's pitching (24–13) could not get the Red Sox higher than second place, and the respective hitting of Tris Speaker (.352) and Ty Cobb (.383) could not bring the Athletics and the Tigers any higher than third and fourth place. The Sox galloped through the league that year, the nearest to their dust was a full nine games back at season's end. Their 100 wins that year is the most a White Sox team has ever posted in a season. With only 54 losses, their .649 percentage is

Art Shires, who had dubbed for himself such nicknames as "The Great" and "What a Man," became just as well-known for the use of his fists as for his baseball skills. Shires on two occasions blackened eyes of then Sox manager Lena Blackburne. He also went into the ring to box Chicago Bears center George Trafton, to whom he lost a 3-round decision. With the Sox he batted .341, .312, and .258 in 2½ seasons (1928–30).

Ted Lyons pitched his only no-hit game for the White Sox August 21, 1926. The victims of the 6–0 rout were the Boston Red Sox.

J. Louis Comiskey, son of the Old Roman, took control of the White Sox in 1931. He headed the organization until his death in 1939.

On August 31, 1926, White Sox second baseman Ray Morehart collected nine hits in a double-header, the first American League player in history to accomplish that feat and still a major league record he shares with eight other players.

Before an exhibition game in 1931, two Chicago pitching greats pose together at Comiskey Park, Red Faber of the Sox (left) and Charlie Root of the Cubs.

Comiskey Park was remodeled and enlarged for the 1927 season. Seating capacity grew to 52,000. The first home run hit in the newly laid-out stadium was from the bat of New York Yankee Lou Gehrig.

Lew Fonseca came to manage the Sox in 1932 after playing with Cincinnati and Philadelphia in the NL and Cleveland in the AL. His three years at the Sox helm were losers, an overall record of 120–198 (.377), but Fonseca had had a fine career as a player. He had a lifetime batting average of .316 with a career high of .369 in 1929.

Ted Lyons pitched all 21 innings for the White Sox May 24, 1929, in a single game at Detroit. The Sox lost the extra-inning affair to the Tigers 6–5.

Sad Sam Jones pitched out the last four years of his long career with the White Sox (1932–35). He appeared in his first major league game in 1914; 22 years later he would boast 229 wins against 217 losses (.513). His career with the Sox was less distinguished, 36 wins, 46 losses (.439).

Two of baseball's all-time greats got together here at Comiskey Park before the first All-Star game back in 1933, Al Simmons and Babe Ruth. Simmons joined the White Sox that year after nine years with the A's. In his three years with the Sox, Simmons batted .331, .344, and .267. His lifetime average is .334, and he had such career highs as .392 (1927) and 36 home runs, 165 RBIs and 152 runs scored (1930). Ruth incidentally hit a two-run homer to help the AL win that first All-Star game 4–2.

Vern Kennedy hurled a no-hitter at Comiskey Park August 31, 1935, the first that a Sox pitcher had thrown at home since 1914. He beat the Cleveland Indians that day 5–0.

Two Sox catchers of 1933: Frank Grube (left) and Charlie Berry.

George "Mule" Haas takes a swing at spring training camp out in Pasadena, California, in 1933. Haas came to the Sox from Philadelphia that year along with Al Simmons and Jimmy Dykes. Haas would end his career five years later with a lifetime average of .292, although his best season with the Sox was a percentage point below that figure. (*World Wide Photos*)

Henry "Zeke" Bonura truly was the first White Sox player to carry a big bat, although this one is somewhat exaggerated. A bona fide Sox slugger, Bonura hit 27 home runs his rookie year (1934) to set a new Sox record, one that would be tied but not broken until 1950.

Luke Appling is to the White Sox what DiMaggio was to the Yankees, Musial to the Cardinals, or Williams to the Red Sox. A Hall of Famer, inducted in 1964, he holds practically all Sox career batting records. From 1930 through 1950 Appling covered shortstop for the Sox. A fine fielder, astute base runner, solid hitter, and team leader, his .310 lifetime average ranks 78th in all-time major league history and only 31 players have ever collected more than his 2,749 hits.

In 1936, Luke Appling put together the longest hitting streak in White Sox history, 27 games. The only other Sox batters to hit safely in 20 or more consecutive games are Guy Curtright, 26 in 1943; Chico Carrasquel, 24 in 1950; Minnie Minoso, 23 in 1955; Sam Mele, 22 in 1953; Roy Sievers, 21 in 1960; and Ken Berry, 20 in 1967. That year Luke Appling also became the first White Sox player ever to win the American League batting crown. His average of .388 that year remains an all-time White Sox high.

In his second year as Sox manager in 1935, Jimmy Dykes shakes hands and exchanges batting orders with Connie Mack, who was then in his 35th year as manager of the Philadelphia A's.

Sox hurler Bill Dietrich pitched a no-hit game June 1, 1937, defeating the St. Louis Browns 8–0.

Luke Sewell had toiled with the Cleveland Indians for 12 years and the Washington Senators for two before joining the White Sox in 1935. One of the most reliable catchers in the league, he played for the Chicagoans for four years in the twilight of his career. His best year with the Sox was 1935 when he hit .285.

Monty Stratton suited up and hurled a pitch
for the Sox before a benefit game for him at
Comiskey Park in 1939. A front-line pitcher
for the Sox, Stratton lost his leg as a result of
a gun accident on a hunting trip the year
before. The Cub player looking on is one of
baseball's all-time great pitchers, Dizzy Dean.

The first night game played at Comiskey
Park was August 14, 1939. The White Sox
beat the St. Louis Browns 5-2.

At the All-Star game of 1939, the American League
squad's oldest pitcher, Ted Lyons, 38, of the White
Sox, poses with the youngest hurler, Bob Feller, 20, of
the Indians.

Bob Elson began broadcasting the play-by-play action for the White Sox on radio back in 1932. His career was a distinguished one, lasting all the way into the 1972 season. Elson, renowned gin rummy player and baseball authority, would come to be known as the "Commander," and he would be honored with a plaque in the Hall of Fame for his services to several generations of baseball fans.

Two stalwarts on the White Sox roster in the late 1930s and early '40s were outfielder Mike Kreevich (left) and first baseman Joe Kuhel. Kreevich, in his six years as a Sox regular, batted over .300 three times and .297 on another occasion. Kuhel tied the Sox home run record of 27 in 1940, and twice scored more than 100 runs in his six-year stint in Chicago.

Ted Lyons as a White Sox pitcher:

Year	Won	Lost	ERA	SO's
1923	2	1	6.35	6
1924	12	11	4.87	52
1925	21	11	3.26	45
1926	18	16	3.01	51
1927	22	14	2.84	71
1928	15	14	3.98	60
1929	14	20	4.10	57
1930	22	15	3.78	69
1931	4	6	4.01	16
1932	10	15	3.28	58
1933	10	21	4.38	74
1934	11	13	4.87	53
1935	15	8	3.02	54
1936	10	13	5.14	48
1937	12	7	4.15	45
1938	9	11	3.70	54
1939	14	6	2.76	65
1940	12	8	3.24	72
1941	12	10	3.70	63
1942	14	6	2.10	50
1943–45	(Military Service)			
1946	1	4	2.32	10
Lifetime	260	230	3.67	1,073

Comedian Joe E. Brown got the call to throw out the first ball on a chilly opening day at Comiskey Park in 1940. He is flanked here by Sox manager Jimmy Dykes (right) and Cleveland Indian chieftain Ossie Vitt.

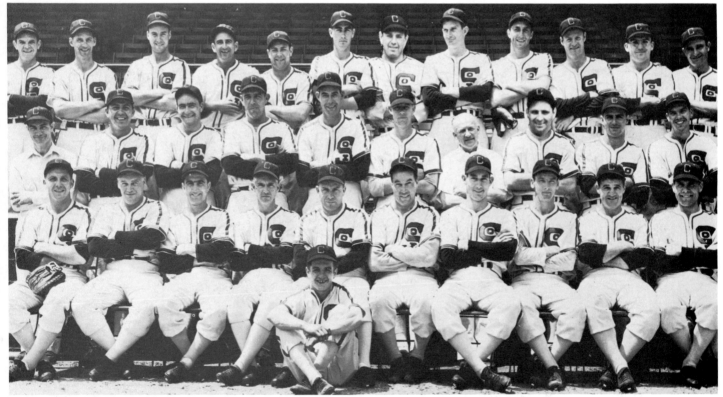

The White Sox of 1941: **Top Row** (left to right)—Myril Hoag, Joe Kuhel, Bob Kennedy, Luke Appling, Taft Wright, Don Kolloway, Ted Lyons, Jack Hallett, John Rigney, John Humphries, Bill Dietrich, Bill Knickerbocker; **Middle Row** (left to right)—Sharkey, Julius Salthers, Tom Turner, Thornton Lee, Monty Stratton, Lee Ross, Dr. Schact, Ben Chapman, Stevens, George Dickey; **Bottom Row** (left to right)— Mike Tresh, Ed Smith, Dario Lodigiani, Ruel, Jim Dykes, George Haas, Joe Haynes, Jimmy Webb, Mike Kreevich, Pete Appleton; **In Front**—Bat Boy, Pete Pervan.

Nellie Fox led the American League in hits during three different seasons—1952 (192), 1957 (196), and 1958 (187). Only one other Sox player has ever led the league in hits, Minnie Minoso in 1960 (184).

From June 1948 to May 1953, Boston Red Sox hurler Ellis Kinder defeated the White Sox 17 consecutive times. His string was broken May 12th when the Sox beat Boston 9-7 in 10 innings.

The greatest Sox second baseman since Eddie Collins was Jacob "Nellie" Fox, who came from the Philadelphia A's in 1950 and remained in Chicago through 1963. A consummate fielder, he holds the major league record for the highest career fielding average (.984). He also holds the major league record for most consecutive games played at second base (798). Fox seldom struck out, and was a true clutch player. Five times he led the league in at bats and four times in total hits. In his 19 years in the majors, Fox played in 2,367 games, batted 9,232 times, hit safely 2,663 times, for a career batting average of .288. Six times he hit over .300.

Manager Paul Richards (center) poses in the Sox dugout in 1951 (his first year at the Sox helm) with two of his moundsmen, Billy Pierce (left) and Randy Gumpert. The Sox would break into the first division (4th place) that year for the first time since 1943.

Jim Busby, the speedy centerfielder of the original Go-Go Sox of 1951, symbolized the kind of racehorse baseball the team would play through the decade. That first year as a regular he batted .283 and stole 26 bases, second only in the American League to Minnie Minoso's 31. The next year Busby would move on to the Senators.

Al Zarilla was brought to Chicago in 1951 to add a little punch to the batting order. Zarilla had played for five years in St. Louis with the Browns and two with the Boston Red Sox. He batted .257 for the Sox that year and contributed 10 homers, then was traded to the Browns the next year.

Saul Rogovin was traded to the Sox by the Detroit Tigers in 1951. That same year he produced 11 wins for the Sox and led the entire American League with an ERA of 2.78. During Rogovin's three years with the White Sox he won 32 games and lost 28 (.533).

Nellie Fox as a White Sox batsman:

Year	Batting Average	2B	3B	HR	RBIs
1950	.247	12	7	0	30
1951	.313	32	12	4	55
1952	.296	25	10	0	39
1953	.285	31	8	3	72
1954	.319	24	8	2	47
1955	.311	28	7	6	59
1956	.296	20	10	4	52
1957	.317	27	8	6	61
1958	.300	21	6	0	49
1959	.306	34	6	2	70
1960	.289	24	10	2	59
1961	.251	11	5	2	51
1962	.267	27	7	2	54
1963	.260	19	0	2	42
Lifetime	.291	335	104	35	740

The White Sox of 1951, the team that won the nickname "Go-Go Sox:" **Top Row** (left to right)—Joe Dobson, Nellie Fox, Gus Niarhos, Phil Masi, Billy Pierce, Harry Dorish, Joe DeMaestri, Don Lenhardt, Hollis Sheely, Ross Grimsley, Jim Busby; **Middle Row** (left to right)—Ken Holcombe, Randy Gumpert, Howie Judson, Bob Boyd, Minnie Minoso, Ed Stewart, Luis Aloma, Saul Rogovin, Lou Kretlow, Esler (trainer); **Bottom Row** (left to right)—Ed Robinson, Floyd Baker, Chico Carrasquel, Jim Adair (coach), Roger Cramer (coach), Paul Richards (manager), Ray Berres (coach), Leon Harris (coach), Ray Coleman, Bob Dillinger, Al Zarilla.

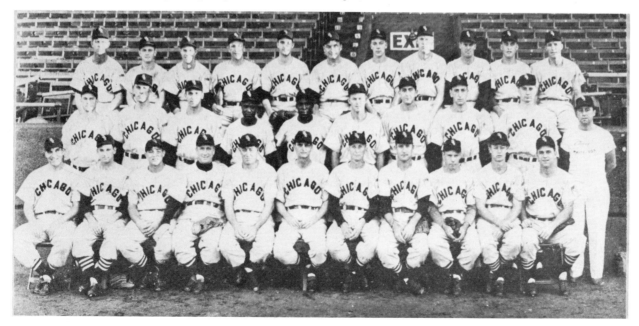

Before a Sox–Cubs exhibition game in 1951, managers Paul Richards (left) and Frankie Frisch pose for the cameras in front of the batting cage at Comiskey Park.

Luis Aloma handled a good portion of the White Sox bullpen duties from 1950 through 1953. A native of Havana, Cuba, he played only with the Sox and ended his career with 18 wins and 3 losses (.857), including 15 saves.

Outfielder Sam Mele was an established hitter when he came to the White Sox to hopefully enrich their poverty-stricken offense in 1952. He stayed through the next season, batting .248 and .274 in those two seasons, but his most memorable feat was the 22-game hitting streak he came up with in 1953, fifth longest in Sox history.

Harry Dorish, who went by the nicknames of "Fritz" and "Chunky," was a mainstay in the Sox bullpen from 1951 into 1955. During that time, he was credited with 36 saves and compiled an overall record of 31 wins and 20 losses (.608).

In a surprise move, brawny Gus Zernial of the Philadelphia A's tries to steal second base, only to be tagged out by former teammate Chico Carrasquel. The throw was from Sox catcher Gus Niarhos.

Lefthander Jack Harshman set an all-time White Sox strikeout record July 25, 1954, when he fanned 16 Red Sox batters in a single game at Boston. The record still stands today. Twice Big Ed Walsh struck out 15 batters in a game, in 1908 and 1910, and Jim Scott got 15 once in 1913.

Virgil "Fireball" Trucks pitched two one-hit shutouts in 1954, beating Boston 3-0 and the Tigers 4-0.

One of the great fielding cornerstones ever, Chico Carrasquel and Nellie Fox, who handled the activities around second base at Comiskey Park from 1950 through 1955.

Nellie Fox became the first Chicago White Sox player ever to be named the American League's Most Valuable Player when he was so honored in 1959. Runner-up for the award that year was Sox shortstop Luis Aparicio.

Early Wynn became the first, and so far only, White Sox pitcher to win the Cy Young Award. He was honored with it in 1959, the year he helped the Sox to a pennant with a record of 22–10 (.688) and an ERA of 3.16. The 256 innings he pitched that year were the most in the American League.

The mighty Ted Kluczewski came to Chicago late in the 1959 regular season to pump some power into the Sox batting order as they made their run at the pennant. The Big Klu came through for them in the World Series when he whacked three home runs, drove in 10 of the team's 23 runs, and batted .391. He batted .293 for the Sox the next year but hit only five homers. For his 15 years in the majors, Kluczewski is credited with 279 home runs and a career average of .298.

Sox outfielder Ken Berry slides safely under the leap of Washington Senators second baseman Bernie Allen in one game in 1967, while Sox infielder Sandy Alomar is not so successful as he tries to get beneath the dancing feet of Baltimore Oriole shortstop Mark Belanger in another game.

One of the game's premier home run hitters, Rocky Colavito brought his bat to Comiskey Park for part of the 1967 season. He only contributed three roundtrippers for the White Sox, but hit a total of 347 in his 14-year career to rank him 24th among all major league home run hitters.

A key member of the White Sox bullpen during the second half of the 1960s was Bob Locker. He contributed 58 saves to White Sox causes during those years, and in 1967 led the major leagues in appearances when he pitched in 77 games.

Sox second baseman Wayne Causey takes a header here as Bobby Knoop of the California Angels tries to break up a double play in this 1967 game at Comiskey Park. Knoop succeeded. Looking on is shortstop Ron Hansen.

Ken Boyer of the Sox dives for first base in this game against the Cleveland Indians. First baseman Tony Horton, with ball in hand, is not quite quick enough to put the tag on Boyer. The other Indian is pitcher Luis Tiant. Boyer only played for the Sox during parts of the 1967 and 1968 seasons. During his 15-year career, spent mostly with the St. Louis Cardinals, he compiled a lifetime average of .287, with a total of 282 home runs and 1,141 RBIs.

Rich "Goose" Gossage began his major league career in Chicago in 1972 and worked in the Sox bullpen through 1976, but his best years would be with the Yankees. As a member of the Sox, Gossage did have one excellent year, however, 1975, when he led both leagues with 26 saves, and produced a 9–8 record and an ERA of 1.84.

Jim Kaat had 14 years experience when he came to the Sox in 1973, including one season when he was the league's ace hurler (1966: 25–13). His first full year with the Sox, 1974, he topped 20 games for the second time (21–13), and followed the next year with a 20–14 season. As a Sox pitcher, in just a little more than two seasons, Kaat won 45 games and lost 28 (.616).

White Sox pitchers Blue Moon Odom and Francisco Barrios combined efforts to pitch a no-hit game against the Oakland A's on July 28, 1976. The Sox won it 2–1.

The White Sox, 1977:

1b	Jim Spencer
2b	Jorge Orta
3b	Eric Soderholm
ss	Alan Bannister
lf	Richie Zisk
cf	Chet Lemon
rf	Ralph Garr
c	Jim Essian
dh	Oscar Gamble
p	Steve Stone
p	Francisco Barrios
p	Chris Knapp
p	Ken Kravec
p	Lerrin LaGrow
Mgr.	Bob Lemon

In 1977, utility infielder Jack Brohamer hit for the cycle—single, double, triple, home run—in a game at Seattle. He is only the second Sox batter to accomplish that, the other being catcher Ray Schalk, who did it against the Tigers back in 1922.

Sox right fielder Pat Kelly dives back to first and both he and the Minnesota Twins' Harmon Killebrew look expectantly for the umpire's call. Kelly was safe on this pickoff attempt by pitcher Bert Blyleven. Kelly played for the Sox from 1971 through 1976; his best year was 1974 when he batted .281 and stole 18 bases.

Brian Downing was back-up catcher to Ed Herrmann in 1973 and 1974, took over the job full time for the next two years, then ceded it to Jim Essian before being traded to the California Angels. There, he would have his best year in 1979, batting .326.

The White Sox drew the largest single season attendance in their history in 1977, a total of 1,657,135.

Terry Forster, a top reliever for the Sox in the early and mid 1970s, is mobbed after one of his 75 saves for the Sox. His two best years in Chicago—1972, when he pulled out 29 games, and 1974, when his 24 saves were the most in the majors.

Sox shortstop Bucky Dent is in the process of completing a double play against the Yankees in 1974. Looking on is former Cub Ron Santo who played the last year of his major league career across town with the Sox. The Yankee base runner is Graig Nettles.

Paul Richards returned to manage the Sox in 1976 at the behest of new owner Bill Veeck. But it was hardly like old times. The Sox had a dismal season, 64–97 (.398), landing in the cellar of the AL West.

Harry Caray was the voice of the White Sox from 1970 through 1981 when he moved across town to broadcast for the Cubs. The "Mayor of Rush Street," as he is also known, had a long career in baseball broadcasting with the St. Louis Cardinals before coming to the Sox.

Jimmy Piersall, color commentator for White Sox broadcasts since 1977, became a key part of the new Sportsvision team instituted in 1981 by the Sox. Always outspoken, often controversial, and most of the time walking a tightrope between the team management and his loyal listening audience, Piersall would fill a variety of roles in telling the Sox story and in commenting on it.

Ralph Garr batted over .300 in three of his five years as a starter for the Atlanta Braves before coming to the Sox in 1976, including a league-leading .353 in 1974. Garr hit exactly .300 in each of his first two years with the Sox, then dropped into the high .200s before being traded in 1979.

Jim Essian was the Sox front-line catcher in 1976 and 1977, then, after a three-year interlude in Oakland, returned to serve as back-up for Carlton Fisk in 1981. Essian's best year was 77 when he hit .273, including 10 home runs.

The Sox first baseman for 1976 and 1977 was Jim Spencer who came from the Texas Rangers and departed the Sox for the Yankees. Spencer tied Jorge Orta with 14 homers in '76 to lead the team, and then hit another 18 the following year.

Lamar Johnson slides to break up a double play in this spring training game against the Pittsburgh Pirates. Leaping over him is second baseman Phil Garner. Johnson joined the Sox in 1974 and has batted over .300 three times since. His top average was .320 in 1976, and the following year he clouted a career-high 18 home runs.

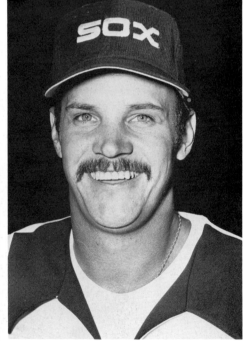

When the Sox needed some power in 1977 they went to the National League for Richie Zisk. It cost them relief pitchers Terry Forster and Goose Gossage, but Zisk whacked 30 home runs and drove in 101 runs that year. They were unable to keep him the following year, however, and Zisk went to the Texas Rangers.

Bill Veeck holds court from a corner of the Bard's Room at Comiskey Park. Veeck's second session as Sox owner lasted from the 1976 season through 1980.

Bob Lemon managed the Sox to a third place finish in 1977, but his team had slumped to fifth the following year when he left for the New York Yankees to replace Billy Martin. For his superb pitching career with the Cleveland Indians (1946–58, 207 wins and 128 losses, .618), Lemon was inducted into the Hall of Fame in 1976.

Oscar Gamble played one year in Chicago, 1977, and, when he wasn't tending to his hair, managed to lead the team in home runs with a total of 31. He also batted .297 and drove in 83 runs while serving much of the time as the club's designated hitter.

Eric Soderholm played the keystone corner for the Sox from 1977 until he was traded in 1979. In his first season he cracked 25 home runs and batted .280; the following year he led the team with 20 fourbaggers.

After a long career with the Cubs, Don Kessinger eventually came to the South Side to play in the Sox infield. He played from 1977 into 1979. That last year he took over as player-manager but was replaced after 106 games, of which his team had won only 46. As a player, Kessinger, in his 16 years in the majors, appeared in 2,078 games and had a career batting average of

Chet Lemon slides for the plate under a high-jumping catcher from the Toronto Blue Jays in this 1978 game. He was safe.

Britt Burns is a product of the free agent draft of 1978. The 6'5" hurler was 19 years old when he made his Sox debut. By 1980 he was a key starter and turned in a fine rookie record of 15–13, with an ERA of 2.84. In '81 he again turned in the best mound performance for the Sox, winning 10 and losing 6 while maintaining a 2.64 ERA.

In 1981, Britt Burns pitched 30 consecutive scoreless innings, the second longest such stint in White Sox history. Billy Pierce holds the record with 33^2_3 scoreless innings in 1955.

Mike Squires has been the Sox first baseman for most of the time since 1979. His best year was 1980 when he hit .283.

Wayne Nordhagen did just about everything for the White Sox in 1979. Here, putting the squash and a tag on a runner, he is a catcher, but he also played in the outfield, pitched two games, and served as designated hitter that year. Nordhagen came up with the Sox in 1976 and hit .315 the next year and .301 the year after, playing in about a third of the games each year. In 1981, he was the Sox' leading hitter, with an average of .308.

Tony LaRussa, arguing here, was managing the Iowa Oaks, a Sox farm club, in 1979 when he got the call to come to Chicago and lead the Sox through the remainder of that season. At 34, he was the youngest manager in the major leagues. Under LaRussa the Sox won 27 and lost 27 in '79, but the following year they could only win 70 for him while losing 90 to end up in fifth place in the AL West. In 1981, in the cumulative standings for the split season the Sox ended up in third place, with a record of 54–52. LaRussa also is an attorney.

Utility infielder Greg Pryor came to the White Sox in 1978. His most fruitful year was 1979 when he batted .275.

Rich Dotson donned a Sox uniform in late 1979 and produced a record of 2–0. The following year he moved into the rotation and won 12 and lost 10. Dotson came up with nine wins against eight losses in 1981.

The Sox traded for infielder Jim Morrison in 1979, and he secured a fulltime job second base in 1980, when this photo was taken. Morrison batted a respectable .283 that year, including 15 home runs. In '81 he moved to third base and batted .235.

Rich Wortham had the best of his three years with the Sox in 1979 when he won 14 and lost 14. He left after the 1980 season.

The 5,000th White Sox home run was hit September 2, 1981 at Comiskey Park by Chet Lemon.

Ed Farmer has been the Sox ace reliefer since 1979 when he was acquired from the Texas Rangers for Eric Soderholm. He saved 14 games for them that first year and then set an all-time Sox record with 30 saves the next year. Farmer's record for 1981 was 3–3, with 10 saves.

The White Sox new owners of 1981, Eddie Einhorn (left) and Jerry Reinsdorf, flank Chicago's mayor Jane Byrne, whom they hope to convert into a loyal baseball fan. (Photo courtesy of the City of Chicago.)

The White Sox picked up Tony Bernazard, completing a double play here, from the Montreal Expos in the winter of 1980. The 24-year-old quickly won the starting job at second base and batted .276 for the Sox in his premiere year.

Chet Lemon was one of the best hitters for the White Sox from 1978 through 1981. He joined the Sox in 1975 and became a regular in center field the following year. He hit .300 or better three times in his last four years, his best effort being in 1979 when he hit .318, including 44 doubles, the league high and only one short of the all-time Sox record. Lemon hit .302 in 1981, and was traded after the season to Detroit for slugging outfielder, Steve Kemp.

Lamarr Hoyt commuted between the White Sox and their farm clubs in 1979 and 1980 before arriving for a full, if abbreviated, season in 1981. That year he won nine and lost only three, with an ERA of 3.22.

A rookie in 1980, Harold Baines found full-time work in right field. He batted .255 that year, and followed in '81 with an average of .286.

Steve "Rainbow" Trout moved from the minors to the Sox in 1979 and promptly won 11 big-league games while losing only 8. He turned around a poor 1980 season (9–16) in 1981 by winning 8 and losing 7.

Shortstop Bill Almon was not even a roster player going into the 1981 season but managed to win a starting job and then turned out a performance as the best-hitting shortstop in baseball that year, with an average of .301.

Acquiring Carlton Fisk, the longtime star catcher for the Red Sox, in 1981, was the first step in upgrading the Sox line-up by new owners Eddie Einhorn and Jerry Reinsdorf. A Rookie of the Year (1972) and a regular in many All-Star games, Fisk holds numerous Red Sox records for batting and fielding. Coming to the Sox, Fisk carried a career average of .284 and a total of 162 homers. His 1981 production for the Sox was below that average output—.263 and seven home runs.

The White Sox got Dennis Lamp from the Cubs in 1981 in exchange for Ken Kravec. Lamp won seven and lost six while posting the club's best ERA in 1981, 2.41.

Greg Luzinski, 6'1", 225 lbs., twice a runner-up for the MVP award when he was with the Phillies in the National League, has been one of the game's premier power hitters since the early 1970s. During his first year with the Sox, 1981, he became the team's focal point, hitting 21 home runs in 106 games and driving in 62 runs, far and away the best slugging effort on the club that year. At the end of the 1981 season Luzinski had 244 career home runs.